MIX
Paper from
responsible sources
FSC® C144853

Published in 2022 by OH!
An Imprint of Welbeck Non-Fiction Limited,
part of Welbeck Publishing Group.
Based in London and Sydney.
www.welbeckpublishing.com

Compilation text © Welbeck Non-Fiction Limited 2022
Design © Welbeck Non-Fiction Limited 2022

Disclaimer:
All trademarks, quotations, company names, registered names,
products, characters, logos and catchphrases used or cited in this book
are the property of their respective owners. Any use of lyrics or song
titles in this book is purely coincidental and incidental and used as
reference or for identity. This book is a publication of *OH!, an imprint
of Welbeck Publishing Group Limited*, and has not been licensed,
approved, sponsored, or endorsed by any person or entity.

All rights reserved. No part of this publication may be reproduced,
stored in a retrieval system, or transmitted in any form or by any
means (including electronic, mechanical, photocopying, recording, or
otherwise) without prior written permission from the publisher.

ISBN 978-1-80069-186-5

Compiled and written by: Lisa Dyer
Editorial: Victoria Godden
Project manager: Russell Porter
Design: Tony Seddon
Production: Jess Brisley

A CIP catalogue record for this book is available from the British Library

Printed in China

10 9 8 7 6 5 4 3 2 1

Illustration: Original photograph by David Fisher/Shutterstock

IF I COULD
TURN BACK TIM

THE LITTLE GUIDE TO

CHER

IF I COULD TURN BACK TIME

CONTENTS

INTRODUCTION

There is simply no one like Cher. A mix of street smart, intelligence, humor, talent, and beauty, she's the celebrities' favorite celebrity and a legend in the world of entertainment. With six decades of No.1 hits, from her Sonny and Cher days to her latest album (number 26) *Gold Dancing Queen* in 2018, to ABBA covers off the back of her starring success in *Mamma Mia! Here We Go Again*, she's reinvented herself again and again.

Turning her hand to serious acting in *Silkwood*, *Mask*, *Moonstruck*, *The Witches of Eastwick*, and more, the multitalented star began a new career in the 1980s, and emerged as the "Goddess of Pop" with dance-oriented pop-rock in the 1990s— gaining a dedicated tribe of gay followers in the process. From LGBTQ+ rights to politics, from saving elephants to TikTok, she's as engaged and relevant as she ever was—and she always has a lot to say for herself.

On the following pages, you will find a collection of the funniest, sharpest, most deadpan quotes you'd expect from this authentic one-of-a-kind diva whose Twitter account *The Guardian* described as "a jewel in the bizarro crown of the internet."

A consummate entertainer, Cher has always been there for her legions of fans, as journalist David Munk says, "like the Statue of Liberty in sequins." Larger than life, she's beloved by generations for always speaking her mind with wit, warmth, and honesty.

CHAPTER
ONE

I GOT YOU, BABE

Cher's Californian
upbringing and the early days
of Sonny and Cher, in her
own words.

My mother was the most creative, fantastic person and would come up with great things for us to do. She'd buy art supplies and all of us would sit around painting. I was lucky.

Out magazine, May 2002

When I grew up, it was a time when women were just supposed to be cute and not have many opinions. My mother and her friends were quite different. They were all the most beautiful women you've ever seen . . . and they were very strong women.

CNN, September 24, 2013

When I was really young, my mom said: 'You're not going to be the smartest, you're not going to be the prettiest. You're not going to be the most talented. But you're going to be special.'

Billboard Music Awards speech, 2017

I was a shy ugly kid who led a big fantasy life. I thought I was an angel sent from heaven, to cure polio. When Dr. Salk did that, I was really pissed off.

People, September 1, 1985

66

When I was young, there was this section in *Reader's Digest*. It was called 'The Most Unforgettable Character I've Ever Met.' And for me that person is Sonny Bono. And no matter how long I live or who I meet in my life, that person will always be Son for me.

99

Eulogy for Sonny Bono, 1988

Sonny and Cher met in 1962 when she was a 16-year-old high-school dropout and he was a 28-year-old assistant to record producer Phil Spector.

When Cher filed for divorce in 1974, she cited "involuntary servitude" as the reason and was left penniless, as Sonny owned 95% of Cher Enterprises with the rest held by their lawyer.

I was this massive amount of energy with no direction. I knew what I wanted to do, but I never would've gotten there without Sonny.

Billboard, May 27, 2017

We were living that song.
Sonny wrote that song for me,
and it was about our life.

About "I Got You Babe", Benjamin Svetkey
interview, 1999

He was my mentor, he was my father, he was my husband, he was my partner, he was my daughter's father. They were all equally important, and so much focus was on the marriage, but the marriage was the least-working thing.

About Sonny, Benjamin Svetkey interview, 1999

Born Cherilyn Sarkisian on May 20, 1946, she released her first solo single under the name Bonnie Jo Mason, and she and Sonny Bono were first known as Caesar and Cleo. She legally changed her name to just "Cher" in 1978.

Everyone hated us. People were frightened of us. They thought we were dirty, because of how we looked. They tried to beat us up.

On being Sonny and Cher, *Billboard*, May 27, 2017

Even if we don't say nice things about each other, it doesn't mean anything. I know Sonny too well.

Biography.com, June 6, 2019

I had such a hero worship of Sonny, long after we were together. I just thought he was great.

Biography.com, June 6, 2019

Originally a platonic relationship, Sonny and Cher grew closer as they sought and found stardom. They had a faux "marriage ceremony" in 1964 (and would officially tie the knot in 1969).

Sonny was the nice guy. I was the b**** that sang well and looked great in clothes.

CBS News, 2013

I was so happy to let him do all that. I was just so uninterested. I designed the clothes and I sang, and I was the inspiration, I was the Muse.

About the Sonny and Cher relationship,
Behind the Music: Cher documentary, 1999

[He treated me] more like
a golden goose than like his
wife . . . I forgive him, I think.

Vanity Fair, November 2010

I think he's screwing with my chandelier. It goes on in the middle of the night when the switch is down—on and off, on and off. And it would just be like him to do that.

On believing her late ex, Sonny Bono, is haunting her, November 6, 2013

We lived a public life. There was no way we were going to get away with a private divorce.

On her divorce from Sonny, *Behind the Music: Cher* documentary, 1999

I would have gone home to my mother, but I'm not that crazy about her either.

After leaving Sonny, J. Randy Taraborrelli's
Cher: The Unauthorized Tell-All Biography, 2021

"

At first all I wanted to be was famous; then I realized that fame had nothing to do with talent. I felt that I didn't do anything quite well enough, that I was one of those people who was famous but not very talented. So I said, okay, I'll be the Dinah Shore of the Seventies, on TV all the time but nobody quite knows why.

"

J. Randy Taraborrelli's *Cher: The Unauthorized Tell-All Biography*, 2021

The Sonny and Cher Comedy Hour was a massive TV hit in the 1970s, sometimes luring 30 million weekly viewers.

The show discontinued when they divorced but was revived for two seasons later in the decade. Both stars had toy dolls made by Mego; Cher's even outsold Barbie in 1976.

CHAPTER
TWO

THE ONE AND ONLY CHER

Famously self-effacing, there's no one as authentically individual as Cher. Here are her thoughts on self-image and superstardom.

I've been the same person since I was six years old. So I don't get that whole reinvention thing.

The Sun, October 12, 2019

I'm a child of the Sixties and
I have this rebellious streak.
I don't want to buckle under to
people who have these ideas
of what is acceptable. The
Academy is not my mother.

Cosmopolitan, February 1988

I'm not a role model, nor have I ever tried to be a role model. The only thing about me as a role model is I've managed to stay here and be working and survive.

IMDB.com

Look, I'm only difficult if you're an idiot. If you don't know more than I know, then I'll be really difficult.

Vanity Fair, November 1990

I don't know what else I would be if I wasn't me. I am not looking from the outside, looking back. I am who I am.

Sydney Morning Herald, September 22, 2013

I always wanted to be famous because I thought that if I couldn't be good [at something], I'd be famous. I was never really good. I was just something different and I got to be famous for being different.

J. Randy Taraborrelli's *Cher: The Unauthorized Tell-All Biography*, 2021

It's not enough to be famous for me. Famous is empty so quickly, it's not what people think it is. It's wonderful, but if you're famous and you feel that you're an artist inside and everyone thinks you're just a celebrity, it's really painful.

To Andy Warhol, *Interview*, March 18, 1982

I don't think that we are born
with a finite number of dreams.
One thing about dreams is that
they can be whatever you want
them to be, you don't have to
put a limit on them, you don't
even have to know them.

V magazine, September 23, 2013

I'm scared to death of being poor. It's like a fat girl who loses 500 pounds but is always fat inside. I grew up poor and will always feel poor inside. It's my pet paranoia.

www.brainyquote.com

Cher wasn't born into privilege or wealth. Her mother, divorced from Cher's Armenian-American truck-driver father, struggled to find work so much that Cher was put into an orphanage for a short time.

66

I never cared about money.
I'm not destined to be a rich
woman. I'm destined to be
a woman who makes a lot of
money and never has any. I've
made millions and millions and
millions of dollars and I just
spend it.

99

Interview, March 18, 1982

I think I am a product of my mother's sensibilities and my mother's values. There has been lots of battling and lots of love and it's never an easy road for us. But in the deepest recesses, I do have my mother's values.

Sydney Morning Herald, September 22, 2013

All of us invent ourselves. Some of us just have more imagination than others.

Time, May 20, 2016

I've been famous my entire life;
I don't know any other way.

www.feelthewords.com

I've always taken risks, and never worried what the world might really think of me.

Time, May 20, 2016

If you really want something
you can figure out how to make
it happen.

Time, May 20, 2016

I don't have confidence. I don't do things out of confidence. I just do them for lack of any other road.

Behind the Music: Cher documentary, 1999

I'm standing backstage frightened out of my mind saying, 'I can't do this.' Then my choreographer tells me, 'If God didn't want you to do this, he wouldn't have looked down on your cradle and said "sequins".'

"

The Oprah Show, May 2008

I don't know what keeps me
down to earth but it isn't ironing.
I send mine out.

www.cherworld.com

I've had high highs and low lows, and you've just gotta keep going. I always think of myself as a bumper car, and if you hit a wall, you go, 'OK, what am I gonna do?' And you back up and you go in another direction. There are endless possibilities.

Paper, February 17, 2016

I've never compromised who I am, not ever. If I've gotten anywhere in my life it's been on my own merits.

Forbes, April 9, 2019

I am the girl who everyone said was never going anywhere. I guess I shocked a few people.

www.azquotes.com

I'm really happy with the peaks and the valleys. It's the valleys that make me, force me, to reach further.

TV Guide, August 1999

Everybody has good things happen and bad things happen, and long stretches where nothing happens at all.

New York Times, September 4, 2018

Until you're ready to look foolish, you'll never have the possibility of being great.

99

Time, May 20, 2016

There are lots of things that I'd like to be, and nice just doesn't seem good enough.

The Oprah Show, 1991

Cher's dyslexic, which she blames for her grammatically challenged tweets.

Erratic capitalizations and wild punctuation, along with plentiful random emojis—the ghost is her favorite but you'll also see sweat droplets, prayer hands, and cake—make her messages a form of visual pop art.

Ipad freezing up! Maybe it's overwhelmed because it Just realized A fabulous DIVA Was touching it! Can't really Blame it, 'SNAP OUT OF IT'

Twitter, March 7, 2013

"

IM NOT YELLING . . . IM CHER

"

In response to the question "WHY ARE YOU ALWAYS
YELLING?", Twitter, June 22, 2016

> **"I'M ALMOST FINISHED WITH ALBUM. THINK IT'S GOOD, & (as we all know) I'M NOT A BIG CHER FAN"**

Twitter, July 25, 2018

CHAPTER
THREE

LOVE AND UNDERSTANDING

She may be famous for her
headline-grabbing romances,
but Cher is warm, funny,
and wise when it comes to
matters of the heart.

I love having boyfriends. A girl can wait for the right man to come along—but in the meantime that doesn't mean she can't have a wonderful time with all the wrong ones.

99

You magazine, *Mail on Sunday*, November 28, 2010

Mother told me a couple of years ago, 'Sweetheart, settle down and marry a rich man.' I said, 'Mom, I am a rich man.'

The Observer, November 26, 1995

66

If you smell like dessert, men won't forget you.

99

On her perfume Eau de Couture, *The Late Late Show*, April 22, 2021

My relationships usually last a few years. When I'm involved with a man, other men are fascinated with me, but the minute I'm single again, half of those men disappear because they don't have the balls to really want me.

New Musical Express, April 1984

"

You gravitate to the people you gravitate to . . . People like who they like. If I was a man we wouldn't even have this conversation. And that sucks out loud.

"

On criticism following her dating of 18-years junior Robert Camilletti, *Behind the Music: Cher* documentary, 1999

Younger men are more supportive and a lot less demanding, and they also have more time for their relationships.

Macleans, March 6, 1989

66

Men aren't necessities. They're luxuries.

99

Jane Pauley interview, *NBC Dateline*, June 27, 1996

You know, honey, husbands come and go but I'm still Cher at the end of the day.

To Christina Aguilera on *Burlesque*, CTV News, November 19, 2010

66

The only grounds for divorce in California are marriage.

99

IMDB.com

Cher's liaisons are legendary. From a brief fling with Warren Beatty when she was 16, she went on to 13 years with Sonny, then a raft of musicians and actors, including music producer David Geffen, second husband Gregg Allman, Tom Cruise, and Val Kilmer, before her great love, "bagel boy" Robert Camilletti.

The trouble with some women
is that they get all excited about
nothing—and then marry him.

BCC *Observer*, February 2005

It's not necessary in order to be a complete person that I have a man. It's not the end-all, be-all of my life.

Time, May 20, 2016

If grass can grow through cement, love can find you at every time in your life.

The Times, May 30, 1998

Try to be in as many
relationships as you can.

On happiness, Extra TV, February 8, 2008

66

I'm still friends with all my exes, apart from my husbands.

99

In Michael Heatley's *Massive Music Moments*, 2008

I trust my friends. They force me to examine myself, encourage me to grow.

www.cherworld.com

Gregory was a southern gentleman who also happened to be a heroin addict.

On her second husband, *Parade*, November 21, 2021

He was possibly the one true love of my life. I hate the phrase 'toy boy'. It's so demeaning. Nobody blinks an eyelid about Michael Douglas marrying Catherine Zeta Jones . . .

On Robert Camilletti, *Women's Realm* via *InStyle*, September 17, 2020

66

Anyone who's a great kisser I'm always interested in.

99

www.quoteopia.com

I wouldn't mind living with someone forever. I don't really want to get married. I don't see any reason for it. And yet I'm so romantic that every time I think I meet someone I want to live with them forever and ever.

Interview, June 12, 2013

I don't need a man. But I'm happier with one. I like to have someone I can touch and squeeze and kiss. But I don't fold up and die if I don't have a man around.

Cosmopolitan, July 1991

There's not someone who tells you how adorable you are and rubs your head and goes into a crowded press conference and stands at the back and winks at you so that you think, 'I can get through this.'

Sun Sentinel, March 28, 1999

66

To me, marriage is for five or ten years.

99

www.azquotes.com

When you stop trying to find the right man and start becoming the right woman, the right man will find his way to you.

Time, May 20, 2016

When Chaz first told me about wanting a sex change, I had a really hard time with it. We talked about the transgendered thing intermittently for years . . . But the press was kinder than I thought they would be.

On her daughter Chaz transitioning, *Parade*, November 21, 2021

I just wanted my daughter to grow up, get married, have children, and get divorced like everyone else.

www.azquotes.com

CHAPTER
FOUR

IT'S ENTERTAINMENT

Variety performer,
contralto chanteuse, movie star,
and pop-culture icon: Cher's
had one of the most multifaceted
careers in showbiz.

I don't think of myself as a singer. I think of myself as an entertainer, and the best place I do it is onstage.

Extra TV, May 20, 2021

I love the way singing feels in my body—because it's so big, and I'm not. But the music comes out in the biggest way.

New York Times, September 4, 2018

The first concert I attended was an Elvis concert when I was eleven. Even at that age he made me realize the tremendous effect a performer could have on an audience.

"

Graceland.com

A lot of the biggest entertainers are shy. I've always been shy. But once I'm on stage and get hold of an audience, I know I can bring the room together as one. No matter how many thousands of people, I can bring it to where they are all friends. If you have a heartbreak or a sickness, for 90 minutes I can make you forget.

The Guardian, December 14, 2020

Cher fronted a rock band, Black Rose, which appeared on the *Tonight Show*, released one album in 1980, and supported Hall & Oates on tour. However, reviews were mixed and the album a commercial failure.

I've had so many rebirths,
I should come with my own
midwife by now.

Pittsburgh Post-Gazette, April 16, 2019

In this business it takes time to be really good—and by that time, you're obsolete.

www.cherworld.com

Some guy said to me, 'Don't you think you're TOO OLD to sing rock n' roll?!' I said, 'You'd better check with Mick Jagger.'

Twitter, November 2, 2018

66

Performers love to perform—
that's the thing that we do.

99

Associated Press, February 17, 2009

Cher's marathon Farewell Tour lasted from June 2002 to April 2005, covering 325 shows, the most ever by a female solo artist, and grossed more than $250 million.

But lucky for her fans, it was no farewell, and she resumed touring with Dressed to Kill in 2014 and Here We Go Again in 2018–20.

Famous people pay a price. Their privacy is invaded—things that would never happen to regular people.

Parade, November 21, 2021

I'm a perfectionist, my own boss.
If someone isn't pulling their
weight, I let them know. I'm a
nice person but you can't say
yes to everyone.

www.cherworld.com

"

My idea, every night before I go onstage, is that this is a gift I was given, and can give to people. While they're watching my show, they don't have to think of anything else. It's something that makes people feel good. That's all I do—make people feel good.

"

Billboard, May 27, 2017

The only female artist in history to have had No.1 singles over six decades, she has sold 100 million records, won an Academy Award, a Grammy, an Emmy, three Golden Globes, and the Best Actress Award at the Cannes Film Festival.

I've been made a joke all my career life. I've been one of the most popular women in America and a joke and somehow inside of me . . . Mike Nichols said to me, 'You know, I should have listened to you when you told me you were talented.'

Interview, March 18, 1982

Some years I'm the coolest thing that ever happened, and then the next year everyone's so over me, and I'm just so past my sell-by date.

Rolling Stone, April 15, 1999

People said I was a huge joke. I've been a joke so many times. I've been on my way out since I started, but I'm strong-willed. My mother is so much tougher than I am and my grandmother is so much tougher than my mother.

IMDB.com

66
The road is a nasty place
and lonely.

99

USA Today, September 17, 2013

"

L.A. is kind of like heroin,
I guess. It seems like it would be
a beautiful, quiet peaceful
feeling and then it kills you.

"

Interview, March 18, 1982

Singing is like going to a
party at someone else's house.
Acting is like having the party
at your house.

Entertainment Weekly, 2010

They thought I wasn't serious. I didn't dress like a serious actress and I had younger boyfriends and they really weren't ready to let me in. It took me 30 years to get a job.

On her acting career, October 25, 2013

In 1982 Cher made her critically acclaimed Broadway debut in Robert Altman's *Come Back to the Five and Dime, Jimmy Dean, Jimmy Dean*, and was nominated for a Golden Globe for her appearance in the film version.

You don't have to be smart to act—look at the outgoing president of the United States.

About Ronald Reagan, 1988, in *Brewer's Cinema*, 1995

Yeah. I wanted to be an actress and everybody said, 'No, you can't, you can't, you can't.' And I just kept saying, 'Oh, I can, I can, I can.' And there were certain things I had to give up to get the chance to do it.

Harlan Jacobson interview, *Film Comment*, January–February 1988

66

Meryl Streep is an acting
machine in the same sense that
a shark is a killing machine.

99

James Park's *Film Yearbook*, 1989

In the 1980s Cher established herself as one of Hollywood's leading ladies with a string of blockbuster films, including *Silkwood* (1983), *The Witches of Eastwick* (1987), and *Moonstruck* (1987), for which she won an Oscar.

I won't be able to do what I'm doing forever. There aren't that many scripts floating around for fifty-year-old chicks.

www.filmbug.com

I haven't a clue why I've lasted so long. There's no reason. There are many people more talented than me. I think it's luck.

IMDB.com

I'm serious about my work, but I don't take myself seriously. I'm not precious, you know.

CBS News, September 22, 2013

66
I'd rather have freedom than fame.

99

Sunday Times, September 22, 2013

I can't listen to my own voice, I don't like it. You see all your mistakes when you hear your voice. You see all your imperfections.

Interview, June 12, 2013

I was so nervous that I couldn't remember where the 'e' was in my name!

On signing her name in cement outside Grauman's Chinese Theatre, November 18, 2010

My gay following has kept me,
in the old days, alive, you know?
When no one else came to see
me. I've had really bad times.

CBS *Sunday Morning*, September 22, 2013

In 1998, at 52, Cher became the oldest woman to have a No.1 hit on *Billboard's* Hot 100 with "Believe", the Grammy Award-winning title track from the album that topped charts around the world, selling 20 million copies.

The song was also notable in that Cher pioneered the use of Auto-Tune to manipulate her voice on it.

CHAPTER
FIVE

BELIEVE

Whether it's LGBTQ+ rights
or politics, Cher's fearless
words show why she's a force
to be reckoned with.

It's not that I can't accept no. I just don't believe it. If I believed no, then I wouldn't be in any of the places that I am.

Vanity Fair, November 1990

I believe what I believe so I don't care. I just say what I want.

Perth Now, October 3, 2013

In my personal life I'm not very tough at all, but in my professional life, having to deal with being a woman in a man's world, I'm really tough. I never back down from a fight or an argument. I'm willing to stand there, toe to toe with anyone.

www.quotenova.net

There should be no bitch fighting. Women should hang together. But girls don't have that one down. And I think some women maybe don't like the idea.

Sydney Morning Herald, September 22, 2013

Don't buy into the idea that women aren't strong enough to do anything they want on their own.

You, Mail on Sunday, November 28, 2010

❝
If you don't take it, no one is
going to give it to you.

❞

Las Vegas Women's March, 2018

This has nothing to do with men, I love men, but until women get paid the same, have control over their bodies, a number of things thought of as equal, then you can't stop.

Sydney Morning Herald, September 22, 2013

It's a rough business, and it's a rough business for women. But it's better now than it was when I started, because it wasn't good at all. Back then, women did not have the opportunity to be their own masters. People wanted to pat you on the head and tell you to go sit in the corner until it was time to sing.

Paper, February 17, 2016

Women have to harness their power—it's absolutely true. It's just learning not to take the first 'no.' If you can't go straight ahead, you go around the corner.

Flatt magazine, February 24, 2014

Yes, it's a man's world, but that's all right because they're making a total mess of it. We're chipping away at their control, taking the parts we want. Some women think it's a difficult task, but it's not.

K1047.com, August 26, 2021

One thing about prejudices—
once you break one of them,
you're screwed, because then
they all have got to go.

Parents, Families and Friends of Lesbians and Gays,
Washington D.C., October 12, 1996

I know I'm not supposed to have any opinions about politics because I'm famous.

Vanity Fair, November 24, 2010

Gay guys like a certain kind of woman. They like a flamboyant woman that's broken. They like a balls-to-the-wall woman, motherly but not; sexual but not. Gay guys are like this: they either love you or they don't even know you're on the planet. Once you have them, you have them.

"

The Guardian, November 7, 2013

I admire anybody for standing up for what they believe—man or woman, I don't care. Having beliefs—especially if other people don't agree with you— it's difficult in this day and age.

Billboard, September 24, 2013

Gay men understand that
I understand what it's like to be
an outsider.

CNN, December 16, 2020

Living your life the way you want to live it is the most important thing so if you have to pay small prices along the way, it's not important.

www.morefamousquotes.com

The only thing in the world
you can change is yourself and
that makes all the difference in
the world.

www.azquotes.com

Cher's has suffered from Epstein-Barr virus, and the chronic fatigue that followed, which sidelined her music and film career in the late 1980s and early 1990s.

For two years she couldn't work and was forced to turn down movie roles and stop touring.

I'm an elitist lib-tard whose grandmother picked cotton, whose mother sang in bars when she was eight years old during the Depression . . . I want to tell you who I am so I can tell you what I believe.

We Stand United Rally speech, New York, 2017

It's not always a happy ending when sometimes you say things that you think, and it goes against the grain of the larger group.

CNN, September 24, 2013

Do you think I would have lasted 48 years if I really gave a flying f*** what people think! I pull up my big-girl G-string, follow my path, and move on.

As seen in *Vogue*, May 20, 2015

66

Don't take your toys inside just because it's raining.

99

www.quotefancy.com

"
I only answer to two people:
Myself and God.

"

Behind the Music: Cher documentary, 1999

Cher is an outspoken advocate for causes ranging from women's rights and LGBT equality to veterans' rights. She is associated with many philanthropic organizations and campaigns, on subjects such as AIDS/HIV, Habitat for Humanity, the Children's Craniofacial Association, and most recently CherCares, an initative for Covid-19 pandemic relief.

Women, unlike most men, are able to accept mystery, accept whatever comes to them—even if it's not logical.

IMDB.com

If you're waiting for someone to believe in you, you'll be waiting forever. You must believe in yourself.

Woman and Home, June 24, 2021

I can't spell or do grammar, but I'm smarter and more serious than people think. I'm no featherweight when it comes to digging deep and being involved. So many stars I know do so much. It's our duty to give back.

USA Today, September 17, 2013

Cher and the Loneliest Elephant was a 2021 Smithsonian Channel documentary about how the multifaceted entertainer fought to move an elephant living alone at the Islamabad Zoo to a Cambodian sanctuary.

I'm just the worst little Buddhist in town.

Vanity Fair, November 24, 2010

I have a problem with religion that makes it so, like, 'We are the ones. We are the chosen ones.'

Vanity Fair, November 24, 2010

Honesty makes me feel powerful in a difficult world.

IMDB.com

Sometimes I don't tell the truth, which is telling the truth about not telling the truth. I think people don't tell the truth when they're afraid that something bad's going to happen if they tell the truth. I say things all the time that I could really get into trouble for, but they kind of blow over.

CNN, September 24, 2013

Stand & B Counted or Sit & B Nothing. Don't Litter, Chew Gum, Walk Past Homeless PPL w/out Smile. [If it] DOESNT MATTER in 5 yrs IT DOESNT MATTER THERE'S ONLY LOVE&FEAR.

Twitter, October 11, 2021

YOU MUST NEVER BECOME NUMB!! Turn Sadness, & immobility into activity & renewed Resolve . . . You must get involved with life Not Shrink from it. If you don't like the way things are Change Them.

Twitter, May 18, 2018

CHAPTER
SIX

IF I COULD TURN BACK TIME

Whatever Cher wears
or doesn't wear, she owns it.
Here are her reflections on
body image, fashion, beauty,
and aging.

I'm insecure about everything, because . . . I'm never going to look in the mirror and see this blond, blue-eyed girl. That is my idea of what I'd like to look like.

99

Vogue, May 20, 2015

66

Going hungry never bothered me—it was having no clothes.

99

www.cherworld.com

> " ... when you dress, you're expressing yourself in whatever way you feel like. You should never be inhibited by what people expect you to do. "

Paper, February 17, 2016

I do stuff with hair and costumes, and things like that, because what am I going to do? Come in a pair of overalls and a white T-shirt? I mean, that would be boring.

The Sun, October 12, 2019

Sometimes I wonder if people clap because I'm still alive, or because I can still get into my costumes.

People, May 7, 2021

You've probably noticed already that I'm dressed like a grown-up . . . I apologize to the Academy, and I promise I will never do it again.

99

72nd Annual Academy Awards, March 26, 2000

>>

I wear my clothes, my clothes don't wear me.

The First Time, 1999

Pushing boundaries in red-carpet fashion since her tummy-baring, sequinned Sixties styles, Cher understood early on that fashion was entertainment.

Aided by her 40-plus-year relationship with designer Bob Mackie, she's pulled off some of the most outrageous outfits, such as the groundbreaking "naked dress" for the 1974 Met Ball.

If I want to put my tits on my back, it's nobody's business but my own.

Vanity Fair, November 24, 2010

I think the longer I look good,
the better gay men feel.

AnOther magazine, April 16, 2015

Ok! Who wants to talk about my AMAZING HAIR!!! Lmao! So many hilarious description! 'Cher's wearing puppies on her head.'

Twitter, June 19, 2013

So far I'm the oldest chick
with the biggest hair and the
littlest costume . . . I have
shoes older than most of
these nominees!

MTV Video Music Awards ceremony, September 12, 2010

Nobody dislikes my age more than me. I can't help it that I've been here this long.

News.com.au, October 3, 2013

A guy said . . . 'What do you do with Cher? She's too old to be young and she's too young to be old.' I can't go the other way, so I'll have to wait 'til I'm old enough to be old.

CBS News, September 22, 2013

I'm the female equivalent of
a counterfeit $20 bill.
Half of what you see is a pretty
good reproduction, the rest
is a fraud.

Doug McClelland's *Star Speak: Hollywood
on Everything*, 1987

I've had my breasts done.
But my breast operations were
a nightmare. They were really
botched in every way.
If anything, they were worse
after than before.

Parade, January 27, 1992

I'm a witch! I sold my soul to the devil. I have a portrait of Dorian Gray in my cupboard.

Extra TV, February 12, 2008

Sometimes I feel like an
old hooker.

New York Times Magazine, October 18, 1987

Nothing lifts me out of a bad mood better than a hard workout on my treadmill. It never fails. Exercise is nothing short of a miracle.

Cher Forever Fit, 1991

I've been screaming at the top of my lungs at my family, 'Work out! Work out! Old age is coming!'

Vanity Fair, November 24, 2010

The truth is, that in my job, becoming old and becoming extinct are one and the same thing.

Mirror, December 12, 2012

Someone once said, 'The only thing that will be left after a nuclear holocaust is Cher and cockroaches.'

Behind the Music: Cher, 1999

I'm going to die wearing the same things that I love wearing. I'm going to wear my jeans. I'm going to wear wifebeaters. I'm going to wear my leather jacket. I don't care. As long as I can look good in it, and feel comfortable in it, then I'm going to do it.

CNN, September 24, 2013

BREAKING NEWS. I'M BEING BURIED IN MY FISHNETS!!

Twitter, March 2, 2015

At 65, you have to retire and go eat dog food or whatever. It's a shame to be discarded because of something that happens to everybody. Old is like an enemy you have to make peace with before you get there.

NewNowNext.com, May 20, 2016

I just don't know how to accept it [aging]; I don't want to, either. But I don't really know how to. I look in the mirror and I see this old lady looking back at me. I have no idea how she got there.

Today, NBC, October 19, 2016

> **"**
> I have done so much more
> than I thought I would do, and
> yet I am not finished.
> **"**

Stargazing.com, May 20, 2016